Small Scars
Jenny Prater

Small Scars
Copyright © 2020 Jenny Prater
All rights reserved. Printed in the United States of America. No part of this book may be used or reproduced without permission except for in critical articles and reviews.

Print ISBN 978-1-952185-02-1
Digital ISNB 978-1-952185-04-5

Cover illustration by Jenny Prater. Cover design and interior layout by Jenny Prater.

Wax Heart Press

Waxheartpress.com
Jennyprater.com

For Adele—
Love you forever.

Contents

White Bear	1
Manic	2
Forget Me Not	3
Cataracts	4
Days Like This	5
When Last	6
I Like You	7
Mystery	8
Love Poem	9
Depression: An Analogy	10
Well	12
Bang	13
Nostalgia	15
What Would People Say	16
Someday	17
Alone	18
I Wish, I Wish	19
Still	20
Goodbye	21
I Don't Talk	22
Miss You	23
Ghosts	24
Wax	25
Dead Things	26
Coyote	27
Hell Bus	28
Happy	30
Frankenstein	31
Cooties	32
Memories	33
Anne	34
Sleep	35
I'm Not Good at Accepting the Inevitable	36
For You	37
Surprise	38
Haunted	39
Crow	41
The Night	42

Heat	43
Enchantment	44
Substitute	45
Winter	46
Cherry Trees	47
Like That	48
Dance	49
Alive	50
Choose	51
The Sun Circles You	52
Hermit	53
Static	54
Everything	55
Glass Houses, Stained	56
Forgetting	57
Language Barriers	58
Better	59
Plan	60
Want	61
Labyrinth	62
Horizon	63
Simple	64
Dead	65
Loved You	66
Beneath the Steeple	67
Hate, Fate	68
Stones	69
Lately	70
Tonight	71
Hurt	72
Sing	73
Frog	74
Graveyard	75
Siren	76
Family: An Exercise in Business	77
Poppy Field	78
Samson	79
Some Nights	80
Packed Away	81
For a Given Value of Love	82

A List of Dreams for Future Days	83
Party	84
The Night the Mermaid Reclaimed Her Voice	85
Not Yet	86
Without You	87

White Bear

I am sitting on the back
Of a paperwhite bear
And he is taking me far, far
Far away from here

Together we fly frozen
Through the sea
Beneath the ice and into dreams

I ride through mountains and valleys
I ride through forests and hills
There is deep thick fur to warm my hands
As we race away to the silver moon

Are you afraid? he asks
No, I am not afraid
No, I say, I am not afraid

For the sky is full of tinsel
And everything is glitter on the ground
And I sit on the back of a paperwhite bear

He stares with shining, forget-me-not eyes
And I sink through fur like a cloud

On the back of the North Wind I've ridden
In an enchanted palace I've slept
And I've danced with the finest of men

But nothing is better than this
And I am not afraid
No, I am not afraid

I ride on the back of a paperwhite bear
And snow falls like sunshine in far away lands

Manic

It's the same sort of euphoria
You felt at your first slumber party
Six years old and high on sugar,
On friendship, on how the world looks
Past midnight

When you're young you call it being hyper
And don't question how it lasts days, or weeks

Once you spend three months strung out
On a giddy sort of unwanted joy
That drives you to push
And push
And push
Against the walls of reality
Until you wake up one morning
And only know which way is up
Because of how damn down you are

It's like jumping without a parachute
And forgetting you'll someday hit the ground

And some days you wish to be normal
To be steady, level all around
When it comes it feels not
Good but right
Addictive, a biological,
Born-with-it drug

The higher you fly, the farther you fall
But it's an awfully pretty feeling
Living up there in the clouds.

Forget Me Not

The first thing I fell for
Was the color of your eyes
A perfect match for perfect skies
Perfect petalled forget-me-not eyes

But I was never a good gardener
Digging dirty fingers into the soil of you
Not meaning to pull you up by the roots

And after everything you smile at me
Like rain in a blue, blue sky
A fox's wedding every time you cry

The sky shines gold in the moments
Before it all goes dark
And I think some days we work the same way
Fleeting perfection just before it falls apart

I'm sorry I couldn't be better for you
I hope you'll find your own way soon
But forget me not, darling,
Forget me not

Cataracts

What's it like, they ask
When you say you're Depressed
And you tell them

It's like cataracts on your soul

It's like the devil made a funhouse mirror
Which shattered and scattered
And pieces are lodged in my mind and my heart

It's like a chemical spill in my ribcage
And everything is
                Just
                        So
                                Far
                                        Away

Days Like This

I think I'm so sad those around me must feel it
Enough excess misery radiating out of me
To depress the whole Midwest
On days like this my voice is flat and robotic
Because it hurts too much to try to sound human and fail
On days like this I stay inside in case the sunlight burns me
On days like this I look in the mirror and don't recognize my face

These are the days when I forget my own name
The days my bones turn to lead and poison me
The days my bones turn to lead and weigh me down
The days I play hide and seek with myself
And I am always It
And I am never found

On days like this there is only sadness
On days like this my sorrow infects the whole town

When Last

When last we spoke
I dropped toads, not jewels
From my unkissed mouth

When last we shared a bed
No gold was gathered beneath your pillow
For I had taken and eaten your firebird heart
And left you asleep, unloved

When last we journeyed side by side
Your seven league boots outstripped me—
I saddled the wind and rode far away

When last I tried to love you openly
When last I dragged my dreams into the day
We stabbed out each other's eyes by mistake

When last I sought you out
A happy ending was beyond our reach
This time when we start over
I'll love you the right way

I Like You

I'm not expecting much of anything
But I like the shape of your lips as you sing
Along on the dance floor dancing with me
Flowing blue velvet and stepping on feet

I like the feeling of your hands at my waist
Your lips when you kiss me and for once
It's not a mistake

I like the way you push me just a bit too far
The not quite dirty jokes you make

I'm not ready for us to be anything
But this is nice and safe
Like the first crush I never had in seventh grade

I didn't expect to, but I like you.

Mystery

Three dozen roses, a mystery to me
On my front porch, bound with shoe strings
I might love you forever, if you told me your name

In fifth grade it was a paper crane
"You're a great friend" inscribed inside
Though I thought I had no friends that year

If you like me please tell me
To my face
The presents are nice
But a mystery man cannot kill
The loneliness flooding me
And I cannot share my secrets
With a friend I don't know

Three dozen white roses
And I'm still here alone

Love Poem

This is not a love poem
Because I am not in love with you
But I'll admit to being fond
Of how your eyes crinkle when you smile
The way your hair is always tangled
And I like how you laugh at me
When I've said something stupid
As if it's a joke we share
And how you hold my hand
When you're nervous or scared

I am not in love with you
At least not much
But I hope you will always be here

Depression: An Analogy

They give you an ocean and a teaspoon. They make you a lumberjack with a blown glass axe. And you just feel trapped.

It's not about saving a princess, this set of impossible tasks. You don't get anything when you're done, except for getting to be done. Except you're never done. You try and you try and you never get anywhere.

Some days I feel like Sisyphus, and my entire self is the rock I can't roll up the hill.

I'm just so tired of being tired.

Imagine this.

You're sitting on the floor surrounded by birdseed. You have to sort it by type, and you can't do anything else, can't even breathe, until it's done. But all the seeds look the same.

Imagine this.

You're sitting in a garden with a bowl full of rose seeds, and you have to plant them based on the color of the flowers they will someday produce.

Imagine this.

An ogre tells you to sort six bushels of chaff, and you don't even know what chaff is. (You don't even know what a bushel is.)

This is how your brain betrays you.

There's some monster living in your head, demanding lonely monotony that never ends. And you want to be the hero but you can't be till you're done, and your heart is filled with unlimited chaff.

I am so sick of being trapped inside myself.

And maybe it's bad because I'm bad, because don't all the good guys have helpful ant friends?

Or maybe it's hard because I am the ogre myself, and also the prince, and possibly the damsel in distress.

So I sort and I sort the stupid seeds, and all I've ever wanted is just to be free.

Well

You are heavy in the heart
For you yourself are the heart
Of a world which longs to be light

Make your wish
Drop your coin

Let it go

I will take it
I will take it all

Let me be your wishing well

Bang

My brother cries himself to sleep. I put on music to drown him out, and to keep myself awake—closing my eyes, I will see Bundt pans and people I once believed loved me, dream an endless litany of apologies my father shouldn't have to make. I've become a weapon in a war I never wanted, and the wrong side is pulling my trigger.

It started with a phone call—no, it started with a stuffed border collie and a box of tissues, a ride home from school and a voice lesson full of dread. But that part of the story is just for me. It started with a phone call.

He waited until he knew I was alone, and he whispered dirty secrets in the receiver, and he thought he could make me hate my dad, but I have only ever hated him.

I cry. My dad cries too. So I don't hate him—it's still a victory for the other side. Hurt a man's child, you hurt him too.

We had to leave home. And it was a home—here is the church, here is the steeple, here are all of God's people. Except for me.

My dad paints cake pans. I cry myself to sleep, and pretend my brother doesn't do the same. I wasn't really alone. It could have been him who took that call. At least if I'm a weapon, he doesn't have to be.

The cake pans we collect are silver. In my dreams they are red, like my father's bloodshot eyes, like my brother's tearstained cheeks, like my mother's face at the height of her righteous fury. And because I am a young and hopeful weapon, newly minted, I try to go home again.

"Don't come back," the new pastor says. "Don't come back."

And I cry, and my father cries, and my mother and my brother. We are a mess of snot and tangled strings, these days. Three months later, when the new pastor dies, I will cry for him too, just me, hours and days of pointless tears. But I do not think I will ever forgive him for pointing me at my family and pulling the trigger.

Bang. The whole place goes up in flames. We sit in the ruins and lick our wounds.

The next man who points me like a gun at the people I love gets a bullet in his own brain. I'm sick of being used.

Nostalgia

My childhood lives in a golden locket
Which never leaves my neck—
I am not the type
To hide precious things away
And I am not the type
To know how to be an adult
Though there are days I try
To be something present and solid
And grown
More than wispy memories
Of oft-skinned knees
And ballet lessons
And playing in the mud

In my dreams there dwells an endless attic
Full of all the things that meant something
To me

Sometimes it is my grandmother's attic
It is never my own
I am fuelled primarily by nostalgia, you know

What Would People Say

Sometimes you wanna walk into the river
In galoshes full of cement
But you're a smart girl; you know you can't
Because what would people say?
What would people say
If they heard you took the easy way out?

Never make scars where someone could see.

What would people say
If they knew you were a mess?
If they knew how dumb you hurt?
What would people say?

Sometimes you wanna walk across a bridge
The short way, and into the water beneath
Sometimes you wanna put a gun against your brain
But what would people say?

You've always been too vain
Some days it saves your life

Someday

Last week at work I caught an ant
On our sterile medical floor,
Released him outside. In college
I did the same with a mouse
Except it was winter
And I knew he would not survive

And I am so sick
Of dead and dying things
Of always being sad
Not because of life
But because of chemicals in my brain

This morning I sat for hours
Among the rose bushes
Searching for something I still can't name
And sucked blood from the tips
Of my fingers, wrecked by thorns

Someday, I tell the roses,
I tell the mouse, I tell the ants
Someday life makes sense

Alone

I used to be the kind of girl
Who had all kinds of friends
On the playground they played tic-tac-toe
To see who got to be with me each day

I used to be the kind of person
That people used to like
Though mostly they liked that I was shy—
Easy to project your favorite personality
On a friend who never speaks

The volume went up, popularity went down
Now I'm alone on every playground

I tried so hard to be what you wanted
Tried to be the perfect friend
I've been your janitor, your secretary, your dictionary
What more do you want?
What else can I give?

So it's over, so it's finished
So there's no more friends for me
I try so hard, but I never get far
Maybe I'm better off alone

I Wish, I Wish

Click your heels, close your eyes
Good things come to a girl who tries

I wish, I wish for a beautiful place
Where rainbows shine and I can find your face

I wish, I wish for a home by the sea
With a boat for you and a dog for me

I wish, I wish
For impossible things
For laughter and sunshine and matching rings

Click your heels
Close your eyes
Good things come
To a girl who tries

Still

It's so stupid
How I ache to call you, still
And tell you about my day
How I count down the hours
Until the next special occasion
When I can text you
Because "Merry Christmas" doesn't sound desperate
And if I'm lucky we'll have a conversation
For ten or fifteen minutes

In elementary school,
On hot summer days we walked downtown
And placed coins on the railroad tracks
Then stepped back as the train roared past
I have a fortune in flattened pennies, still
Each one worth a different memory of you

In middle school,
We went to the river at the edge of town
And swam in muddy water
Staining the once white polka dots on our suits
And our mothers despaired

In high school,
We took midnight picnics on the hill behind your house
Counting stars and trading promises
And you've broken every one

Some Saturday mornings
My feet still lead me to your parents' house
Near your birthday
I still catch myself at your favorite stores

I still forget
It's so stupid—I still forget
You don't love me anymore

Goodbye

The river is waiting, for me, for me
The trees are all singing, to me, to me
Come back, they say, come back to us
To the wood
It is waiting for me
It is calling to me, to me
But I will not go

The past is gone, the wood is yesterday
I'll say goodbye, I'll say goodbye
The trees have died, the river dried
I'll say goodbye, I'll say goodbye

I Don't Talk

And if words were just words I could speak
This poem every day but I am alone
Grasping fragments of sound in the night
Everything jumbled, crowded and empty and
Too much
And I don't know how to escape

Sometimes the sky is clear and words drop
Like diamonds from my mouth but more often
I speak frogs and snakes and hide again while
shame
Pours down like rain on my head
And I don't know how to escape

My voice peters out as my mouth is sewn shut
And it hurts so much

If my words were my own I would give them to
you

Miss You

Stains on the carpet, bright red
They'll fade to brown soon
They'll fade away
But they'll leave behind
The memory
Of everything you never
Had the chance to be
You're always too young
You're always too young
No matter how old you become

I miss you

Ghosts

We all grow up with ghosts
Most of them our own
Such careless children
Spare parts cast aside
Lost in the wind, lost to time

Don't worry—they'll come back

The pieces you left in your childhood home
Have grown and created lives of their own
And the man who first broke your heart,
He still has a part
Which like a starfish leg has become a whole

I like to meet my ghosts in early evening
When they're weak and still faded from the sun
Too late at night it isn't safe
To see who you could have been

Wax

I loved you in the dead of night
Candle wax dripping down
Candle wax staining your nightgown
Your sleeping face flawless
Until you woke and saw my betrayal

I looked on you in moonlight
A face I thought I'd never see
A promise, promise broken
And then you disappeared

I tried to wash away my sin
Tried to scrub your nightgown clean
But no amount of laundry
Could bring you back to me

I thought if I loved you you'd never leave
But I've chased you, chased you away from me

Dead Things

The fish don't swim here anymore
The snakes don't slither, the birds don't soar
I remember, I think
When things were alive
But it's so far away now—
The world has died
And I'm stuck here inside a place
For dead things
Corpses and horse heads and flies without wings

I will escape, though—I am alive
My wings may be broken but I can still fly

Coyote

There's a coyote dying in a ditch, tire tracks across his back, and I'm running late for your wedding.

Twenty years ago we heard them howl, sitting on the floor beneath your bedroom window late at night, until your neighbor the pig farmer came out with his gun. I don't remember if we mourned them.

Twenty years ago we were wild things, small and savage and sweet, and I never thought we would ever be tamed.

Your new beginning doesn't need to be something else's end, but our friendship has stumbled and staggered through ever-harder years, and I fear your thrown bouquet will be its last gasping breath.

You still mean so much to me: mud pies and tin can telephones, cops and robbers and tiny red spiders we counted as they crawled across our feet.

And I haven't learned to be anything but that half-wild child who howls at the moon, and I know someday soon we'll live only in each other's memories.

Please remember wherever you live your life, I once loved you with all of mine.

Hell Bus

The sky is orange. The lights of the bus glow faintly green. We boarded an hour ago, a day ago, we've been here a thousand years. There have been no road signs for miles.

"Where are we?" we whisper. "Where are we?"
We are on the road to purgatory.

The driver is a middle aged woman with a nametag—Sharon. She does not look at us. She does not speak. Her eyes, if she has them, may be on the road. But we cannot see her eyes from here, her mouth, her face. We cannot see here. We cannot see.

Trees line the road, black, dark blue, but never green. In the night sky all is silent, and none of us can breathe.

"Where are we?" we whisper. "Where are we?"
We are on the road to purgatory.

The air is tainted with the smell of vomit, and we hear faint crying, though it comes from none of us. The bus goes over three potholes. One girl shrieks, but Sharon does not react. None of us react.

Where are we? Where are we?
We are on the road to purgatory.

It seems past time for the sun to rise, but none of us wear watches, and all our phones are dead. Everything is dead.

In the windows we can see the past. Light reflecting on the road, what went behind us looms ahead. And everything is dead now, everything is dead.

We whisper back and forth in endless night, our voices harsh against green light.

"Where are we?" we whisper. "Where are we?" We are on the road to purgatory.

All we are is ash and tar, happy endings gone horribly wrong. We are on the road, on the road. We are on the road to hell.

Happy

We used to wade in the canal
At the edge of the woods
Muddy to our knees
We caught dragonflies and toads
Collected rocks with hints of glittering quartz
And we were happy

We used to play tag in the parking lot
Of the school down the street
On weekends when it was empty
We tripped over each other's feet and fell
Skinning our knees
And scarring dents of pebbles into our palms
And we were happy

We used to climb to the roof of the abandoned church
Downtown on summer evenings
Where we could see the fireworks but not hear them
Making stories for each shape
Making plans for our futures
And we were happy

I thought we were happy
I was happy; what were you?

Frankenstein

It's storming tonight.
It seems it's always storming lately
Like some fucking metaphor
For how my life is spinning
Out of control, and I like it
The steady unending storm
Something comforting
In the danger of it
One thing I can rely on for sure

And you stand in the dark
Getting soaked, catching cold
Hear the thunder rumbling
The taste of electricity in the air
And you hope that maybe
Just maybe
A lightning strike
Will bring you back to life

Cooties

They say it's a phase you'll grow out of
Say you'll grow into love
But you're almost twenty five now
You're nearly twenty five
And it's been ten, fifteen years of this
Ever since puberty hit

They say you haven't met the right guy yet
But it's not as if you've never been
In love
You've met the boy.
You know him and you want him
Bad
But only above the waist

And everyone promises
It's only a phase

It barely makes you sad
The boy you'll never have
He's perfect.
He deserves a full bodied love

But damn how you wish
Some days
You weren't so ace

Memories

My favorite memories
Are of the week before we got the table
Sitting on cushions on the kitchen floor
Drinking apple juice
And eating spaghetti out of teacups
Because the dishwasher was broken

We memorized the cracks in our new ceiling
And traded secrets about our childhoods
And every night we played Marco Polo
In our windowless bedroom
Finding each other again and again

We've been here for seven years
But our house will never be as much a home
As it was those first nights on the kitchen floor

Anne

There's an abandoned playhouse two doors down from my parents' place, and on hot summer days the curtains move in a nonexistent breeze.

I call the ghost Anne.

One summer she possessed me—butterflies in my belly, and nothing else. I named them Want, and Despair, and Need.

They say Anne's body killed her. They say her stomach, empty, rose up and swallowed her whole.

The summer she possessed me, I watched faded paint chip from her playhouse. I skipped rope while I waited for her to devour me from the inside out.

The summer Anne possessed me, I skinned my knees and watched blood pool in my socks. The summer she possessed me, the sky was always cloudless, empty like the body we shared.

When September ended there was cider and pie, and that night I heard the playhouse door slam closed.

In the morning Anne took her butterflies home.

Sleep

Give me a sleeping beauty sleep
Hide my body away
Where my rest will be peaceful and deep
Send no true love's kiss to wake me
I would rather sleep like the dead and besides
There is no true love
For me, I am safe
To sleep forever kissless
Stab that spindle in my heart and it will never
Leave a mark on a target made of stone
There is no love for me, there is no love for me
So let me sleep instead

I'm Not Good at Accepting the Inevitable, and I Refuse to Apologize for That

I am the girl
With a handful of worms
After a heavy rain
Because I know they'll die
When the gutters run dry
Unless I return them to the earth

And I am not the type
To let things go

Snakes in my pockets
Birds in my hands
Metallic black wasp in my room last night
Caught in a cup, released outside

I am not the girl
Who lets things die

For You

I'd sell my soul for tapioca pudding,
Your favorite kind
And half-finished puzzles on the kitchen floor

Some things are worth an awful lot
But love, you're worth so much more

I'd make any deal with any evil
To give you this:
Hopscotch in the parking lot
Climbed trees, skinned knees
Bruises from children's games instead of needles
Nosebleeds from mis-kicked soccer balls,
Not well-placed fists

I'd give anything for your gap-toothed smile
Chocolate on your chin, mischief in your eyes
For those summer days in a happy haze
Of you and me and freedom

Surprise

I've spent half the time I've known you
Waiting for you to die
And somehow it's still a surprise

The cancer crept from your liver
Into the marrow, into your soul
Last time we met you were a stranger
Last time we met I knew it would be the last time
But somehow the loss is still a surprise

One month, my dad said
The last time I asked him
And from then you made it one day

You've always existed, for me
More in stories than memories
But I hoped to know you long enough
To give that a chance to change

It doesn't seem to matter
How long it takes
It always takes me by surprise

Haunted

You commit the murder in May
And they call to say "Wait!
You have more money to pay"

You pay

In June the emails start:
You owe the deceased thirty dollars
You owe the deceased thirty dollars
Your payment is overdue

You ignore this
For six months you are free

In December you hear from a distant friend:
A letter has come to my home
It says you owe six hundred dollars
The deceased demands its due

You call to complain
This is not the ghost I murdered
This is nothing to do with me

And they ask how then does it know your name?
And you have nothing to say

In February your mother calls:
The ghost has come to my house
It wants you to pay

And you call again and again they say:
You have a debt to pay

And you tell them:
I sent my victim debtless to the grave
This bill is not mine to pay

And they say it does not matter
You cancelled your cable subscription—
Now you will never be free

Crow

There's a dead crow in the bushes.

It's the kind of day where anxiety twists up and down your spine, setting off every nerve. The kind of day where you snap at the people you love not because you're angry but because you're afraid of the dark, even when the sun is out.

You're walking home with your little brother and Chinese takeout, counting cracks in the sidewalk, and there's a dead crow in the bushes.

Once, at seven, you got lost in the hills behind your grandmother's house, searching for caterpillars. Instead, you found an ancient car in an abandoned shed, filled, bizarrely, to its cracked windows with lumps of coal. Your mother collected you before night fell, and carried you slowly home.

Later that summer your grandmother died. The funeral was followed by a butterfly with broken wings, which landed on the flowered grave, and never flew away. You cried not for your grandmother, a woman you barely knew, but for things that have forgotten how to fly.

Some mornings you wake sure you're still lost in those hills.

Your brother stumbles at the curb, catching himself before he spills the food. He started a new semester three days ago, and he hasn't learned his roommates' names.

There's a dead crow in the bushes; you turn away to tease your brother.

The Night

The night
Is far
From over
And you used to think
That could be a good thing
But now you are wiser
Now you are older
Now you've learned
To be afraid

And in the dark
They come for you
Pastel nightmares
Whispers of
Forgotten things
A set of hopes
And dreams
You allowed to slip
Away

And this time you know
They're here to stay

Heat

The a/c is broken and you are lost
Lost in the middle of an unmade bed
In the middle of an unending summer
Ceiling fan spinning away but never making your life
Just one degree cooler
All the lights off and all the windows open
And you are lost, lost, feeling nothing but the heat

Lost in a memory you can't quite remember
Like you can't remember the way food sat in your stomach
Back when you ate
Like you can't remember the muscles it takes to make your mouth smile
Though they all say it's easier than a frown
The way you've forgotten the sight of the sky
The smell of the grass
The way it felt to feel a breeze
Before the a/c broke and you got lost
Lost in the endless summer heat

Enchantment

I only love you in the light of day
Rippling fur and shining black eyes
My savior, heavy-pawed

At night the enchantment breaks
I don't know you, small man
In the dark, in my bed
I don't know you,
I don't want to

I fell for a Beast
And I'll fight for a Beast
Spare me this strange, insipid thing
That calls itself a prince

I wanted you.
Not a throne, not a face
In perfect symmetry
That smiles at me without its eyes

Dear, don't let me break the spell
I want imperfect you

Substitute

The new girl comes
And the teacher asks you to show her around
And you do because really, what else do you have going on?
And she asks you to come see a movie
And she asks you to come to the mall
And at a slumber party she does your makeup
After you paint her nails
And looking back two decades later
You still don't know quite what you did wrong

One day you'll find her in homeroom
And the friendship will just be gone
Because she found someone in science class
Who—I don't know—
Knows that nine is too old for Barbies?
Knows that loving your parents is lame?
Someone who wasn't around before.

And it'll happen again when you're twenty
Like it happened at fifteen, at seven, at twelve
You're never really quite good enough
But you'll always do for now

Winter

It's winter now
And I don't know how
To be anything but empty

Families die, children cry
People lie, and the snow
It won't come down

Love is a confusing thing
One part duty, one part nostalgia
All parts quiet
Until the loss

And the world is cold now
Cold in the air
Cold in the ground
Cold inside my bones
And I wish my heart
Was warm enough
To mourn the way I should

No meaningful memories to share
As they put you in the dirt
Just this icy feeling
That everything is wrong

Because we were never close
But you were always there
And this winter you are gone

Cherry Trees

The cherry trees are blooming
Blossoming pink and white and green
The cherry trees are blooming
And we sit at peace beneath

Last summer I traded skinned knees for bouquets
Last summer I traded our friendship for love

Today the cherry trees bloom
And this spring we've relearned
How to be ourselves
Trading giggles and kisses in dew damp grass
Watching the clouds and holding hands

We've set aside our grown-up dates
Instead we're playing hide and seek
And you find me every time

The cherry trees bloom, and blow out, and fall
And on silken petals beneath, we love

Like That

I never used to think about
The color of your lips
(Unremarkable)
Or the shape of your hands
(Long, knobby, a little calloused)
About the just-exposed skin at the small of your back
(Like all the other skin you have)
Or the sound of your laugh
(Like any other laugh)

Until I noticed in a novel
(And another and another)
How the love interest's hair
Falls into his eyes just so
The crinkles when he smiles
The veins in his wrist
Things the protagonist sees so quickly

I never noticed how you smelled
Or the sound of your steps
I've tried to decide the color of your eyes
But it's awkward, all that staring
And I didn't think, before,
About the softness of your skin
About how it glows in the sun
And frankly I still don't care

I love you

I love you
I love you
I love you
But not like that.
I guess I don't love you like that.

Dance

Chalk your hands up
First.
(Dancers don't get blisters)

The only life you learned to live
Was one unflinching, on a stage

Do your makeup
Right.
(The stage lights don't know
You're a little girl)

You grew up just behind the curtain
Memorized the steps

And you'll always do everything backwards
The way you learned in mirrors
The reflection your only teacher
Those long lonely years when you
Were still a girl

Alive

Sometimes I think dying
Is a part of growing up
Maybe it's just the depression
But I used to be wild
And hurting and angry
But lately all I feel is empty
And I want the hurting back

People long to be rid of pain
But at least it's something—
What I would give to hurt

I think I'm a maiden cursed
Because I only feel alive at night
When the sun is hidden from the sky
And I'm trapped in my tower alone
Like the girls who are flowers in the day,
Themselves beneath the stars
Like the man who is a bear until the lights go out
Like the swan who in the moonlight
Can be a princess again

At night I am alive
But in the day,
Well.

I would rather be a vampire
Walking into the break of day
Than a lovely statue on a sun-kissed hill

Choose

They keep telling me love is a choice
But I've tried so hard
To choose to love you
And I can't

I feel with you
Like coral for sale at a beachside store
A perfectly shaped memory
Of what I'm supposed to be
But cold, and hard, and dead

I think of you in the shadows
And try hard to cast a light
But the Lord has not given me matches

I want so much to want you
To see sunlight in your smile
I wish I wished
For the grace of your touch
I wish I knew
How to dissolve in your hands

They tell me love is a choice
You must know if I knew what to do
I would only ever choose you

The Sun Circles You

I sit in the grass beneath the sun
And think of you
You in the morning, barely awake
You in the sunset, with golden-cast skin
You in the evening, giddy and glad

Each stitch in the cross-stitch is vital
But you are the picture, whole

In frosted glass no reflection is cast
Except for yours

Galileo was wrong
The sun circles you

Hermit

I read somewhere that no hermit crab
Begins its life in captivity
That all are caught at the edge of the sea
That every crab once knew what it was to be free
And I try to imagine what it must be like
Until I realize I already know
What it is to be gripped tight by some monster
With thick gloves and beady eyes behind a pair
Of square black glasses who smiles big and
frightening

To be dumped somewhere new as if you should be
grateful
Look at all you have, a ten gallon box of sand
And I used to think that I should be grateful too
For kisses and whispers in a king sized bed

But I came from a life where all the sky was mine
And now a speckled ceiling and puke brown walls
Are here to hold me in, and I used to dip my feet
In the sea and sometimes feel small scuttling
feet
Run across them, before a man ran by and swept
them up
In a net to be sold at some pet store a thousand
miles
Away, before you stole the sea from the fish,
The footprints from my toes, before you stole me
From my heart, and left it rotting on a beach
alone

Static

Used to wake up in the morning
Before TV existed
Those lonely early hours
When everything was static

They say you can't dream in color
Say you can't dream of phones or screens
Guess I've always dreamed
Exactly what I want to dream—
Screw all the rules

Because so many of my dreams
Are of sitting in front of a childhood TV
And static, always static

There's a particular kind of loneliness
To those mornings on the couch
Knowing the world is on pause
Empty but always temporary
A kind of loneliness that's almost glad

Everything

You are merely a memory to me
Blurred out face and a constant skinned knee
The left I believe
Shouting and laughing and jumping off swings
Singing and fighting and pledging the flag
And all the things you've meant to me
Whispers in Sunday school
Angels in snow
Picking the flowers and climbing the trees
Hot dogs and ice cream and memories
I flip through each day and wish I could shake

Now you are a fuzzy, faded face
But once, once
Once you were everything

Glass Houses, Stained

Stained glass windows fill your home
This old church life is all you've known
Hide and seek in the baptismal tank
Hosts of angels with coat hanger wings
And you are the baby of the family,
The body of God

Birthday cakes in the sanctuary
Cheers for small voices that can't really sing
But nothing lasts

The world looks bad through uncolored glass
And you are left with only one request:
Pray for me

Forgetting

I have forgotten the color of your eyes
But the rest I will always remember

The way your hair stuck up in the morning like horns
The way your jeans hung just too low
And your socks were always full of holes

The way you never said what needed to be said
But I'd always know what you meant
And the way your kisses fell feather-light
On all the parts of me I thought were only mine

How you said the meanest things you didn't mean
And raised one eyebrow and laughed at me
The way I still see you in every dream

I am forgetting and forgetting and forgetting
But I think I still know
The important things

Language Barrier

Your fingers, along my ribs
Your palms, against my hips
Your lips, upon my lips

You say you're talking with your hands
But it's a language I've never learned
How touch means more than touch
How every brushing-up is code for something else

I don't know what secrets you've told me
When no words have left your mouth
I don't know what my body tells you
In this language it can't understand

Better

You say you're doing better
And it isn't a lie
But it's not quite the truth
Because Better is all
You know how to do

You have to be better
You have to be thinner
You have to be better
You have to work harder

You have to work harder
You'll sleep when you're dead

You have to be better
You have to go farther
You have to be better
Can't have marks on your skin
You have to be better
Bleed out the bad

You have to be better
You have to be better

It's not quite the truth
But it isn't a lie
You've been doing Better
You're Perfectly Fine

Plan

I've always wanted a lot of things
But so far I've spent adulthood
Making cookie cutter dreams
And never putting anything
Into the oven to bake

I haven't yet prepared myself
To shift ideas to reality
Honestly
I thought I'd be dead by now.

I never thought I'd need to know
How to make what I imagined true
No one cares what plans you plan
When you never plan to see them through

Want

I want to touch the sun
I want those wings of wax
I want to melt away

I want to hear the singing sky,
To dance with puzzled gulls,
To plummet and feel the world go green

I want to see the heat of heaven
I want to see its heart
I want to watch the dark dissolve

I want to fly, to taste the sky
I want to touch the sun

Labyrinth

I only dream in labyrinths
How can I not?
When in the daylight I am always lost

I can never make sense
Of things that make sense
When life is so full

Of twists and turns and secrets
Which are something I can understand

I am searching for something
I cannot describe
Buried treasure or a new place to hide

But never the exit
Where the world opens wide

I am not ready to be free of the tangled webs
Full of secrets and lies
Not ready to find who I am in the light

One right, two lefts, keep going straight
Through hopes and secrets, past promises
You don't know how to make

I am searching for something
I cannot say what it is or why

I only dream in labyrinths
And I can never quite decide
Am I the hero brave?

Or am I the monster in the middle of the maze?

Horizon

There are streaks of crimson in the sunset
Like blood smeared across the sky
And I should be doing homework
But every cloud has a pinkish lining

The sky's bright blue has faded to periwinkle
And I can just make out a theater mask
In the shadowed translucent half moon

What is left of the sun on the horizon burns
Like it knows this is its last half hour
As tentacles of darkness are reaching out
From the other side of the world

And for a moment I am afraid it will not return
tomorrow

Simple

In the days when we still shared a bed
I thought our lives could be simple

A golden cross around my neck
A silver watch upon your wrist
I would wear dresses
And you would wear suits
And magically I would be a good cook

Our tablecloths would be made of lace
And we'd drink milk, unpasteurized
From depression glass in pink and green

It occurs to me, slowly,
That I imagined for us my great-grandmother's life
And maybe that is why we died

Dead

Lately I've been losing hair
Lately I've been noticing
How bad my body is
Not in the way I used to
When it seemed too big and gross
But in the way malnourished children
Never grow quite as tall

I killed myself once—
Starvation, you know
The body shrinks
One day at a time
And it never quite comes back
Turns out it never quite comes back

The hair is never as thick again
The nails never as strong
My stomach rebels at breakfast
And anything with grease will go wrong

I was never strong
But I used to be stronger,
Used to have a body that worked

I killed myself
But now I'm alive
In a body that has already died

Loved You

I loved you the first time
Playing red rover
That moment you asked them
To send me—me—right over
And I didn't quite try
To break through your arms
Because I wanted so bad to be wanted

I loved you because you loved me
Or claimed to
Giggles and whispers behind frosted glass
I fell in love with being loved

I loved you
I loved you
I loved you
Because you asked

Beneath the Steeple

Sometimes I'm tempted
To carve crosses in my skin
To remind myself Who I belong to
But I know You wouldn't like that

Some days I long so much
To cut myself up—
Small scars to remind you who you are
All the ways you're broken
All the ways you're loved

You can make yourself so many things
When no one else is watching
I can make myself
And break myself
In a thousand little ways

In my soul I sleep beneath a steeple
Though in my body I'm safe in bed
A steeple's sharp, you know
A steeple could pierce your heart
A cross could crush your bones

Though I know it didn't crush Yours

God I try so hard
Beneath the steeple
All I've ever wanted is to be Good
And all I've ever been is good enough

I only want to be better
I only make myself worse
Lord take all my small scars
Here beneath the steeple

Hate, Fate

Every time I'm happy I hurt
And I hate it
Everything I love I lose
And I hate it

And you
You spinners that spin
You weavers that weave
You who cut the thread

I'm coming soon
To dig your graves

I have loved
And I have lost
And it was not better,
Not at all

I asked for a story
But you spun me a lie
And I don't know some days
Why I bother to try
And I hate it
And I hate it and I hate it

Stones

Skin and bones, sticks and stones
And stones
All we are is skipping stones
And I thought at one time
That I might survive
But the only cure for loneliness is love

And I skim the water and the love is gone
And the love is gone

I wonder what the tear ducts do
When your eyes are all dried out
And I wonder what I mean to you
When all is said and done

And maybe you thought I'd skip farther
And maybe I wasn't meant to sink
And maybe I'm thinking
What I want to think
Alone at the bottom of a stagnant pool
Alone at the bottom away from you

And the only cure for loneliness is love
The only cure for loneliness is love

Lately

Lately I've been making rag dolls
Floppy friends from forgotten dreams
My prom dress is now a girl named Amy
Pink silk with brass button eyes
My graduation gown is a boy named John
With delicate stitching down the side

Lately I've been making patchwork
Quilts composed of memories
Stitching all my hopeless hopes
Into something I can touch and see

Lately I've been knitting scarves
Soft wool and second chances

All I know how to make is heartbreak
But lately I'm trying something new

Tonight

Sit on the stoop and tell me your secrets
Sit on the stoop and tell me your fears
Sit on the stoop beneath the stars
Tonight in the quiet the world is ours

Wander down sidewalks beneath midnight skies
Remember when promises were more than just lies
We've traded our daydreams for long faded scars
But tonight in the quiet the world is ours

In darkness we whisper our hopes and our fears
In starlight we leave off our day to day lives
We'll always chase dreams of lost hopeless things
But tonight in the quiet the world is ours

Hurt

She's even smaller than you, they say
And it's not supposed to hurt
(you're better now, you get food down
You know it shouldn't hurt)
But you have always been the smallest
(stomach flu, third grade
you've never been the same—
stomach gone flat, never came back)
And you liked it
You can't remember ever wanting
To be anything but skinny
And you eat your food
And you try so hard
But it's never enough
Because it's always too much
Because you've always been the smallest
And you know it shouldn't hurt
But it does

Sing

We walk barefoot
In the sun with songs
Above us sung out loud
Overgrown grass
Swaying in the breeze
And we need we need
We need—something
But what remains a mystery
So we shrug and dance and sing
We are bloody useless used up things
But today we feel the rising joy
Today we feel and live and sing

Frog

The first frog I kissed
Was never a prince
Nor the next but you—
But you
One wrong move
And I'm not just the girl
Who does cute quirky things
Like kissing amphibians
No now I've got a stupid king

Why can't you let me be?

I didn't want a fairy tale
This was never my daydream
I went to that pond for other things
Muddy shoes and dirt-streaked knees
Cuts and bruises, bugs to see
I go on adventures and find strange things
I am scrapes and scabs
Not dances and glittering dreams
I've never been happy sedate and clean

I'm sorry I kissed you
Please set me free

Graveyard

The air is thick with sadness
And I choke on the ghosts
Of babies, never born
And I trip over the memories
Of grandmothers, dead too soon

My memories are become a graveyard
Tombstones wherever I turn
I miss you in the morning
And beneath the setting sun
I miss you in the crowded halls
And in my bed alone

I don't know how to be without you
But I'll never replace you, my love
I promise I'd rather be alone
Than bloom into another man's hands
While you watch from above or below

Darling I miss you, I miss you, come back to life soon

Siren

My silver tongue is rusted
So let me have a try or two
To find the words that you deserve

It isn't easy, love

I live wrapped in shadows of used-to-be
 And could-have-been
And all the ways I've failed you

There are a lot of things I meant to tell you
Before you left
A lot of sights you should have seen

You could come back, you know

I'll say it like a promise
But we both know it's a lie:
Come swim with me in the wine-dark sea
And this time I won't change my mind

Family: An Exercise in Bitterness

I am mostly convinced that growing up
Largely means losing the people you love

I used to have a whole handful of families
People to fight for, people to trust

How could you hurt me when I love you so much?

Sometimes I meet strangers in the street who ask
"Jenny, do you remember me?"
And I don't know what to say

Sixteen is not young enough to forget a family face
And eleven is not young enough
For memories of affection to fade

But the you I knew would never
Have ditched me for seven years
So maybe I remembered wrong

No, I don't know you
I think I never did

Poppy Field

My lost love lies in a poppy field
In the shadow of the mountain king's home
I found his body—though not his soul—
And placed him there where none would dare
To steal him away again

I don't know where to find the rest of him
Don't know what gate of hell to storm
What cloud to find heaven through
On which ancient ferry to catch a ride

So in this poppy field I forever lie
In the shadow of where we fought
For a life that now you will never live
Darling, darling,
I'll wait for you forever here
In the flowers at the foot of the mountain

Samson

You
With your Hercules body
And your Rapunzel hair
Diamond eyes and silly lies
You make me want to believe

I could have loved you once,
In another world

Adonis face, Atalanta thighs
So cute but your Achilles heel
Is every word you speak
"My mom worked for the CIA"
"I can backflip over a moving car"
"My uncle was married to Marilyn Monroe
But it's a secret"

It's a secret, a secret
It's always a secret, don't check your facts

So cute but you're pathological
Babe I just don't have the time
To sort the truth from all your lies

Some Nights

Some nights I tell my roommates
I'm going to bed early
And it's a lie

Some nights I sit alone on a too-large bed
In flowered leggings and the shirt
That has been my favorite for fourteen years
And I listen to the music I listened to
When I was fourteen, and I cry

Some nights I feel so alone
With the cat curled at my feet
With my friends just one closed door away

Some nights I think I don't know how
To be a person, think maybe I've faked it
Somehow for over twenty years

And I slip into slippers I chose in ninth grade
And I slip into the fingerless gloves
I thought were so cool back then
Though now I only think they're itchy

And I try to slip into
A person I used to be
Two versions of me connected
Through a dozen years and change
By a pointless pain I thought back then
Would some night soon fade away

Packed Away

The summer before I moved away
We baked our feelings
Chocolate chip cookies and confetti cake
Oven always on through the oppressive heat

While the timer ran we spread out on the carpet
Beneath the window where the air conditioner lived
Breathing in dust and fumes
And distantly, vanilla from across the house

I left a week before my father
To start a new school
And you and your family helped him pack—
You wrote me messages on every box

Last winter I moved out
Packed my life into cardboard boxes,
Fifteen years old
And found memories scrawled on every surface
In your little girl print

Someday when my life is unpacked again
I think I'll frame those boxes
And hang them on my kitchen walls

For a Given Value of Love

I love you
As much as I know how to
Which is to say
I prefer your company
Over lonely days
And I enjoy the gifts you bring

I find love in the dictionary
It tells me "affection"
I find affection in the dictionary
It tells me "love"

I suppose I feel affection for you
When you're here
Though I hardly think of you
When you're gone

I love you, I do,
As much as I know how to
As much as I love anyone else

A List of Dreams for Future Days

Someday it won't hurt to wake in the morning
And find myself alive
Someday food won't be a struggle
Someday I won't be alone in the sky
Fighting the urge to chop off golden curls
Someday all the marks I've made on myself will fade
Someday I'll stand amid a crowd and feel safe

Someday

Someday the smile won't chip from my face
Like polish from my nails
Someday I'll find a voice that works every night
The time will come when I know I'm alive
By more than my heartbeat
When I won't see despair in the lines of my hands
When the grass grows green again

Someday
I won't need a list of somedays
Just to get me through today

Party

The summer before seventh grade
We had a sleepover party
The last co-ed extravaganza
Before the parents declared us too old
It was the party where my brother cracked open his skull
On a plastic sword
And where I dyed my hair black by accident

In the last week of college
I attended a party
In my roommate's boyfriend's dorm
And I stumbled barefoot in a gray slip dress
Drunk and dizzy on the ambience
More than on my single jello shot,
Tangled in memories of you

There are so many things I could tell you
But I don't know how to find you anymore

I loved you in the lonely, desperate way
You only feel for your first friend
And these days I half believe
You must have been imaginary

In fairy stories the one you want to never let go
Changes into a snake, a spider, a bear
And you have to always hold on

But I hadn't read those stories yet
In the winter you left,
Growing up in an unexpected direction,
And I didn't know how to follow

My dreams are still an endless party
Fairy revels with us at the center
In a land where we never grow up

The Night the Mermaid Reclaimed Her Voice

The night the prince said yes to another woman
The mermaid sat at the edge of the motel pool
Frozen by a late fall chill

The night he left her
The mermaid screamed at the burned out street lights
Testing the voice he'd once tried to steal

The night her prince said yes
She danced on broken ankles
Thinking of how he never listened
All those days she used to yell

The night he left her
She plunged a knife in the pool to shatter the ice
She shucked off the trappings of the life he led
And dived naked into the ice cold chlorine

The mermaid left man
With prayers for another soon-to-be-broken girl

When the prince said yes
The mermaid swam home

Not Yet

I have looked into the eyes of Death
And Death has said "not yet"
I have seen Death face to face
And Death has told me "not today."

All my life is like the leaves of a barren tree
Lost, this season, lost to me
Become a playground for someone else
And I don't know how to save myself
When who I am is mixed
With so many other long-lost things
Yes, I am become a barren tree

I have seen Death at the break of day
And Death has whispered "run away"

I have made myself a scarecrow scared
Of all of life and unprepared
For any wind that blows my way
Frozen, posted on a post
Surrounded by those who should fear me most

I will be a cloud someday
Drifting and lost, but content that way
I will be a beautiful, fragile, untouchable thing
Far from the world, and free to be me
 I will see Death face to face
And I will tell him "not today"

Without You

Maybe it gets better
Maybe it gets worse
Without you it gets worse
Without you it all fades away
The stars go first

We're sitting on the hood of my dad's red car
In denim shorts and ratty t-shirts
Licking apple juice popsicles
Staring at the sky
In the brief Minnesota summer heat
Talking quietly about nothing

Without you there is nothing
And the stars go first
And the popsicle drips sticky
Down my lonely little girl arm
And the sounds of our brothers
In the backyard always yelling—
Suddenly there's only silence
And the car dissolves beneath me
And I'm sitting on the pavement in the parking lot
Of the place that used to be our home

Without you life is this
So please don't go

www.ingramcontent.com/pod-product-compliance
Lightning Source LLC
Chambersburg PA
CBHW062035120526
44592CB00036B/2140